Come into the Ark with Noah

AN ACTION RHYME BOOK

K235

Abingdon Press

Come into the Ark with Noah

Stephanie Jeffs and Chris Saunderson

Hammer, hammer!
We're banging in nails.
We're building an ark, with Noah.

Bang fist on fist

Listen, listen!
We're hearing a voice.
We're listening to God, with Noah.

Cup hand behind ear

Prowl like a lion

Roar! Roar!
We're searching for lions.
We're looking for lions, with Noah.

Reach forward with out-stretched arms

Swing! Swing!
We're hunting wild creatures.
We're searching for monkeys, with Noah.

Hands facing downwards, wiggle fingers

Tickle! Tickle!
We've found two big spiders.
Bring them in the ark, with Noah.

Hoppity hop!
We're jumping on board
With all of the creatures, and Noah.

Hop like a frog

Rock, rock!
The water is rising.
We're floating on water, with Noah.

Move body from side to side

Open, open!
We're looking outside.
We're looking for land, with Noah.

Push outwards with hands

Join thumbs and wave fingers

Flutter, flutter!
We're finding a dove.
We're setting him free, with Noah.

Take, take!
The dove's found a leaf.
Take it out of his beak, with Noah.

Pick up imaginary leaf

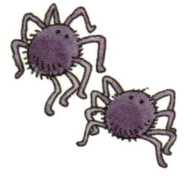

Published in the United States of America by

Abingdon Press

201 Eighth Avenue South

Nashville, TN 37203

ISBN 0 687 04791 9

First edition 2001

Copyright © AD Publishing Services Ltd

1 Churchgates, The Wilderness,

Berkhamsted, Herts HP4 2UB

Illustrations copyright © 2001 Chris Saunderson

All rights reserved

Printed and bound in Malta